The Rainflock Sings Again

The Rainflock Sings Again

Poems by L. Ward Abel

The Rainflock Sings Again
Copyright © 2019 L. Ward Abel
All Rights Reserved
Published by Unsolicited Press
Printed in the United States of America.
First Edition: December 2018

All rights reserved. Printed in the United States of America. No part of this book may be used or reproduced in any manner whatsoever without written permission except in the case of brief quotations embodied in critical articles or reviews.

Attention schools and businesses: for discounted copies on large orders, please contact the publisher directly.

For information contact:
Unsolicited Press
Portland, Oregon
www.unsolicitedpress.com
orders@unsolicitedpress.com
619-354-8005

Some Poems were Previously Published:
Pendora Magazine: "Immaculata," "Sleep, Words, Noises"
The Machinery: "Upriver Cloud to Cloud"
Poetry Repairs: "At Dragonfly"

Book and Cover design by Nathaniel Burgell
Editor: S.R. Stewart

ISBN: 978-1-947021-78-5

10 9 8 7 6 5 4 3 2 1

Contents

Trilogy: Birds	9
Ghost Over Woods	12
Haralson	13
Immaculata	14
Passing through the Grove	15
The Fields	16
Upriver Cloud to Cloud	17
Sleep, Words, Noises	18
At Dragonfly	19
At Shimmer Gap	20
Blades	21
Election	22
Names	23
Dragonfly Meadow	24
In an Effort to Fly	25
Move	26
About the Author	27
About the Press	28

But when the August weather breaks
　　And rains begin, and brittle frost
　　　　Sharpens the bird-abandoned air,
　　　　　　Her worried summer look is lost

------Philip Larkin

Trilogy: Birds

The Angels Rage Tonight
in overflowing amber chutes,
their eyes are Roman camps
their emerald features burn
like peace.

Sky evens in the wake
its heart of blue and white
pulses with cyclical storms
flash now and to come.

Amoretti trade their trip to
Memphis for downriver
where oceans live where dreams
ride summer breezes full of thunder

the sound of currents and birds,
a memory of inhaling rain. The
angels rage tonight alright. There is
singing between keys.

By They Who Piled High Clouds
who stormed through redness through
sounds like mortars mount
magnolia green and orange

and gray
at the end of these Zeusian
holy days through which they

who remember the holiness of jazz
through muted horns before
morning certain lightning blooms it's
on wallpaper, darkness
way down in the lake of birds
below the gap, the clouds

the undergrowth above
through a world that holds
a breathing waits for
sunrise who down now ending
billow they flash above morningtree
Mount Rushmore remnant reset.

Those Above My Line of Sight
birds—and the like—move
so fast as to blur this
wide angle bright view

like messages they flit
golden, flinching and
flexing at the thought of philosophy
of nano-therapy

because it's all figured, shown
understood in the wake
of moving-on but not deeply
there is no need if already known

still I would fly like that if I could
but it is a bog that keeps my
details in the fore I would fly
like that if I could

notwithstanding brevity's own child
the quick tensing that everything
brings is all worth it as
it would seem a flawless stone.

Ghost Over Woods

There's a ghost over the woods tonight.
He knows the dew point.
There is the music again.
I can only seed and cover with earth
a little rectangular trace, but he
gardens wherever it is morning.
Past the point, he dissipates against my
remaining.

Haralson

Red rust to turquoise spreads before it can find a clasping
disheartened from a rhythm of red clay
the streams calcify.

Chopin entertains a night of muted flashing
dreams' refrain he is frozen where ivory has a zip codex
a mind inlaid with butterflies.

The bank lines we cut make staffs and sheets and quakes
unstilled fermenting but discolored now
where the green used to be
they say it evens.

The blue and black east our evening
roofless brick walls
unmarked but for the planets
who eavesdrop.

Don't unsex my countryside
of its dialect, its foliage
its truth be told
just leave alone the way that blood goes out
to all other matters.

Immaculata

The rain is leery of jagged edges.
A blur, she wears salt and shakes like a
watched pot where our star is falling.
A brightening of swallows passes through.
Watershed awnings of riverbed shale
spread-eagle to the elements. See her clay blood,
her green immaculata. See the devil's wife.

Passing through the Grove

What rainy season there has been
is a broken jar shattered
on a painted gray floor
shardened
in a cavern
of doves.

So be it, the way of things,
there would be flattening lines
without our hearing thunder. And
there are local reports of silent
flashes; we may or may not
delight in the roar of the coming
times of storm.

The Fields

On my back porch
screened-in
to shield and to shelter,
the door has fallen off.

So now there is no border,
no line. Yesterday a small bird flew in,
got lost coming to rest
on a palmetto.

Cornered then guided.
I helped him. He darted, a rope
out into the fields, a hay colored bolt
leaving me here in dreamlike tow.

Upriver Cloud to Cloud

She sings "Dust on the Bible"
at the overlook. The sun is
going down in polite
but scattered applause
all orange. Someone should
paint this.

A storm rakes
upriver cloud to cloud;
it's only a backdrop because
it will die out
long before getting too far west.
The next one I think she wrote.

Her songs
reach conclusions.
They are gathered to resemble
birds and geography. Frontiers
blend into homes and then open
space she sings something like
a sparrow that has fallen.

Sleep, Words, Noises

I.
Those words that come when I am half fading
will never be taken down. Soon the eyes
filter away infrared and the jade spectrum
in exchange for characters.

Like the first real sleep in a hundred nights
those dreams can blind you. A color set
a hovering off-white clarity soon gives way
the taste of paradox

still fresh when I wake. Then, my own tell-all to myself
roams a deafening mind. I toil in the holy vineyard.
I sing in a secret place and wait for rumbles
prequels to quietness, to flight.

II.
Look at my dry land, dusty forks in every road
around here no choice appealing, all
directions drop lower to diminished rivers running
backwards in the New Madrid fashion.

Sure enough here at Dragonfly it is too far from
the coronations at Scone where patterns
happen only in hindsight's rise-and-fall of things.
But not in the noisy, simple face of practice
before a post-war where I fly to dream.

At Dragonfly

Here at Dragonfly
I make mention. But
nobody is listening
from towers around the
wide clearing bounces
sounds bespeaking gardens
way off the grid.
It looks like this
whether I am here or not.

Sun betrays treeline
merging slowly dozing into view
an evening blue white to
yellow red and night. Then
green again. Who is the angel
with fire behind? Her condensation trail
scrolls west. Nothing breathes,
my town of storms
belies a shelter from the virus
that is theirs.

At Shimmer Gap

Rolls, wrinkles, ranges
the air is as thin as topsoil
draped over a lake.

The wind always sounds.
Its birds, though informed, still
way beyond caring for me or politics
or a culture of wings and gills

or a Springer's footfall
inhaling commotion whether
mine or hers or theirs. Slick
ponding below mimics those red trees.

There are no doors up here, only gaps.
A vagueness replays, imbeds
makes me discard, edit.
I shun other heartbeats for my own.

I swim down, chutes drop
then return to me from the sky
each fold wakes goes back to sleep
wakes and repeats the thing.

And who understands the absent words?
A few leaves fly the dotted air.
Fluxes juke-flow side to left.
But I have started to rely on things that stay.

Blades

(to Raymond Carver)

Surplus turkey-buzzards
along with greater cousins
seek a new path
to the waterfall

as their living-off carrion
has lost its charm.
My father will be 89
this year.

Sometimes he cuts grass
in shapes of no
particular form
just to confuse us.

His timber fence
has turned gray, his flakes
after almost ninety winters
racing to be mulch.

But those who circle above
had best know their limits
because blades have been
sharpened.

Election

The sun is blue behind the hurricane, its redshift
greened by rain. I have let the grove go
again. So I am giving back what belongs to cicada
choirs of my husbandry. Swing down God
to our graying, swoop low and give us
either peace in the absence or clarity.
Now cometh the eyewall.

Names

When this deluge no longer has a given name
the motives of the conquerors will not matter
nor the sins, nor the sinners.

The Gulf tonight spills round and through
the great salt river miles wide miles deep
blueness surpassing blueness.

Here nighting red white lights go dark
sometimes green back and forth. They
blink like powerline towers here and gone.

Shoreline overgrown and feathered, frayed but
unbroken, winds comb old veins
anonymous and almost flying.

The naming of storms feels
like humanization.
But these storms
are not like us.

Dragonfly Meadow

Reddening, the woods show
survivors at a middlemarch
freeze and display what is coming;
the canvas shudders some
with the force of wings.

Morning clad Rivanna
russet mantle, early glare
gilded Klimtish, then the day;
they settle down and hear a
bell from somewhere.

Noises, Ontario horns
a thousand ponds below
turn away return the breath;
the stir, this little flow
a retaken and held
Palmyra.

www.ingramcontent.com/pod-product-compliance
Lightning Source LLC
Chambersburg PA
CBHW030136100526
44591CB00009B/692

Dedicated with love in every word to the memory of my beautiful and feisty mother, Blanche. My abiding gratitude to everyone who continues to encourage and inspire my writing – my daughters, Margot and Gabrielle, my grandson Alexi, and my dear friends, loves and poetry critique group members. Thank you for allowing me to have other eyes on my work, a hand on my back and arms around my waist.

Contents

my sweet old typist	1
after I have dreamed	3
When the clown came	4
Poem with first line from e.e. cummings	5
I have found what you are like	6
Poem after e.e. cummings	7
sometimes I am alive because with	8
e.e. cummings and I both had uncles named Sol	9
Poem with a line from e.e. cummings	10
Poem with first line from e.e. cummings	11
Poem with a first line from e.e. cummings	12
November Silence	13
somewhere i have never traveled, gladly beyond	14
if i should sleep with a lady called death	15
I carry this stone	16
acknowledgments	19
about the author	21